William J. Standiford

FIRST-TIME HOMEBUYER'S

ULTIMATE GUIDE

Contents:

Welcome Message

Welcome to the First Time Homebuyer's Ultimate Guide! Whether you're ready to embark on this exciting journey of homeownership or just exploring the possibility, this guide is designed to provide you with invaluable insights and guidance every step of the way.

As a dedicated real estate professional, I understand that buying your first home is a significant milestone in your life. It represents not only a major financial investment but also the foundation of your dreams and aspirations. My goal with this guide is to equip you with the knowledge and confidence needed to navigate the homebuying process seamlessly.

Throughout these pages, you will find a wealth of information, tips, and resources to help you make well-informed decisions. From assessing your readiness and creating a budget to finding the perfect home and closing the deal, we will cover every aspect of the homebuying journey.

Importance of Homeownership

Owning a home is much more than just a financial transaction—it's a key that unlocks countless possibilities. Homeownership brings with it a sense of security, stability, and pride. Here are a few reasons why owning a home is essential and often a top priority for many individuals and families:

1. **Building Equity:** Unlike renting, where monthly payments offer no return on investment, homeownership allows you to build equity over time. As you pay down your mortgage, you gradually gain ownership of your property, creating a valuable asset for your future.

2. **Stability and Roots:** Owning a home provides a stable environment for you and your family. It fosters a sense of belonging and community, allowing you to establish roots and become an integral part of the neighborhood.
3. **Personalization and Freedom:** When you own a home, you have the freedom to personalize it to your liking. From interior design choices to landscaping decisions, you can create a space that truly reflects your taste and personality.
4. **Tax Benefits:** Homeownership offers several tax advantages, such as deducting mortgage interest and property taxes, which can lead to significant savings during tax season.
5. **Investment Potential:** Real estate has historically been a sound investment. As property values appreciate over time, your home can become a valuable asset that contributes to your overall financial portfolio.

About the Author & Reading this Book:

Hello, dear readers! I'm thrilled to have the opportunity to share a little glimpse into my world with you. My name is William Standiford, and I am a passionate writer and explorer of the boundless realms of imagination. I was born in Phoenix, Arizona and raised in Farmington, Missouri.

Throughout my life, I've worn many hats - from student to professional, traveler to dreamer - and each experience has shaped the stories I weave. I've wandered through the pages of history, dabbled in the realms of science fiction, and explored the intricate emotions of human relationships.

As it stands, I am an entrepreneur, business owner, and a Real Estate agent! In my free time I enjoy writing, singing, hiking, and building meaningful connections within the community. I enjoy listening to people's stories…it's interesting to see where people have been, what they've endured, and how they've triumphed in their personal and professional lives!

As you embark on this exciting journey, remember that you're not alone. As your trusted real estate advisor, I am here to guide you every step of the way. Together, we will work towards finding the perfect home that suits your needs, lifestyle, and budget.

Let's dive into the world of homeownership and make your dream of owning a home a reality! Feel free to reach out to me with any questions or concerns. I am thrilled to be a part of this significant moment in your life.

Happy reading and best wishes on your home buying journey!

Willy Standiford
Real Estate Agent
Keller Williams STL
Direct: (660) 234-4261
Office: (314) 677-6000

Assessing Your Readiness

Before diving into the process of buying your first home, it's crucial to assess your readiness for homeownership. This involves considering both financial and emotional aspects to ensure that you're well-prepared for this significant step in your life. Let's explore the key factors to evaluate:

Financial Readiness

1. **Stable Income:** Evaluate your employment situation to ensure you have a stable source of income. Lenders typically look for a consistent income history to assess your ability to make mortgage payments.
2. **Credit Score:** Check your credit score and review your credit report. A good credit score is essential for qualifying for a mortgage and securing favorable interest rates.
3. **Savings and Down Payment:** Determine how much you have saved for a down payment and closing costs. While it's possible to find loan options with lower down payments, having a substantial down payment can open up more choices and potentially lead to better loan terms.
4. **Monthly Budget:** Create a detailed monthly budget to understand your current expenses and how much you can comfortably allocate towards homeownership costs, including mortgage, property taxes, insurance, and maintenance.
5. **Pre-approval:** Consider getting pre-approved for a mortgage before starting your home search. Pre-approval not only demonstrates your seriousness as a buyer but also gives you a clear idea of your budget and helps streamline the buying process.

Emotional Preparedness

1. **Long-Term Commitment:** Homeownership is a long-term commitment, and it's essential to be ready for the responsibilities that come with it, such as maintenance, repairs, and ongoing costs.
2. **Stability and Future Plans:** Evaluate your future plans and whether you intend to stay in the area for an extended period. Buying a home makes the most sense when you plan to remain in the property for several years.
3. **Flexibility:** Owning a home can limit your flexibility to move as easily as renting. Consider whether your lifestyle and career allow for a more settled living situation.

Understanding Your Needs and Wants

1. **Must-Have Features:** Make a list of non-negotiable features your ideal home must have. This could include the number of bedrooms and bathrooms, location, proximity to schools or work, and specific amenities.
2. **Desirable Features:** Create a separate list of features you'd like to have but are not deal-breakers. This could include a backyard, a spacious kitchen, or a garage.
3. **Future Growth:** Consider your future needs when choosing a home. If you plan to start a family or work from home, think about how the property will accommodate these changes.

Assessing your readiness for homeownership is a critical step that sets the foundation for a successful home buying journey. Once you feel confident about your financial and emotional preparedness and understand your needs and wants, you'll be well-equipped to find the perfect home that fits your lifestyle and aspirations.

Creating a Budget

One of the most crucial steps in the homebuying process is creating a budget. Understanding your financial situation and determining how much you can comfortably afford will guide your home search and ensure a successful and stress-free experience. Let's dive into the key aspects of creating a budget for your first home:

Determining Your Budget

1. **Evaluate Your Finances:** Begin by assessing your current financial situation. Calculate your total income and factor in any other sources of revenue you may have.
2. **Track Your Expenses:** Review your monthly expenses, including bills, groceries, transportation, entertainment, and any other recurring costs. This will give you a clear understanding of your spending habits and how much you can allocate towards housing expenses.
3. **Establish a Savings Plan:** If you haven't already, start saving for a down payment and closing costs. Having a savings plan in place will help you reach your homeownership goals more effectively.

Calculating Affordability

1. **Front-End and Back-End Ratios:** Lenders often use front-end and back-end ratios to determine how much mortgage you can afford. The front-end ratio calculates the percentage of your income that will go towards housing expenses (e.g., mortgage, insurance, taxes), while the back-end ratio considers all debt payments along with housing expenses.
2. **Rule of Thumb:** A common rule of thumb is that your monthly housing costs should not exceed 28% to 30% of your gross monthly income, and your total debt-to-income ratio should be below 36%.

Keep these guidelines in mind when calculating your budget.

3. **Pre-Approval Amount:** Getting pre-approved for a mortgage will give you a clearer picture of the loan amount you qualify for. It's essential to ensure that the pre-approved amount aligns with your budget and doesn't strain your finances.

Consideration of Additional Costs

1. **Property Taxes:** Take into account property taxes, which can vary depending on the location of the home. Your lender can provide estimates of property taxes for properties you are considering.
2. **Homeowners Insurance:** Homeowners insurance is essential for protecting your investment. Obtain quotes from insurance providers to include this cost in your budget.
3. **Private Mortgage Insurance (PMI):** If your down payment is less than 20% of the purchase price, you may be required to pay PMI. Factor in this additional cost if applicable.
4. **Maintenance and Repairs:** Owning a home comes with ongoing maintenance and potential repair costs. It's wise to set aside funds for these expenses in your budget.

Creating a comprehensive budget will empower you to make informed decisions and narrow down your home search to properties that fit comfortably within your financial capabilities. Additionally, having a well-defined budget will demonstrate to sellers that you are a serious and qualified buyer.

In the next section, we'll explore the benefits of getting pre-approved for a mortgage and how it can give you a competitive edge in the real estate market. Let's continue our journey towards homeownership!

Mortgage Pre-Approval

Congratulations on taking the first steps towards homeownership! One of the most important milestones in the homebuying process is obtaining a mortgage pre-approval. In this chapter, we'll explore the benefits of getting pre-approved for a mortgage, help you understand different mortgage options, and guide you in choosing the right mortgage lender for your needs.

Benefits of Pre-Approval

1. **Know Your Budget:** A mortgage pre-approval will give you a clear idea of the loan amount you qualify for. This helps you set a realistic budget and focus your home search on properties within your price range.
2. **Boost Your Confidence:** Pre-approval demonstrates to sellers that you are a serious and qualified buyer. It can give you a competitive edge in a competitive real estate market, especially in multiple offer situations.

3. **Faster Closing Process:** Since much of the documentation and verification process is completed during pre-approval, you can expedite the closing process once you find the right home.
4. **Identify and Resolve Issues:** During pre-approval, lenders review your credit, income, and financial history. This provides an opportunity to address any potential issues or errors in your credit report.

Understanding Mortgage Options

1. **Fixed-Rate Mortgage:** A fixed-rate mortgage offers a stable interest rate over the life of the loan. This means your monthly mortgage payments remain consistent, providing predictability and ease of budgeting.
2. **Adjustable-Rate Mortgage (ARM):** An ARM starts with a lower interest rate for a specific period (e.g., 5 years), after which the rate may adjust periodically based on market conditions. ARMs can be beneficial if you plan to move or refinance before the rate adjusts.
3. **FHA Loans:** Backed by the Federal Housing Administration, FHA loans are designed for first-time homebuyers and require a lower down payment (typically 3.5%). They are an excellent option for buyers with limited funds for a down payment.
4. **VA Loans:** Available to eligible veterans and active-duty military personnel, VA loans offer competitive interest rates and require no down payment.
5. **USDA Loans:** Designed for properties in eligible rural areas, USDA loans offer low to no down payment options for qualified borrowers.

Choosing the Right Mortgage Lender

1. **Shop Around:** It's essential to compare mortgage rates and terms from different lenders to find the best fit for your financial situation.
2. **Consider Customer Service:** Look for a lender with excellent customer service and responsiveness. You'll want a lender who communicates clearly and assists you throughout the process.
3. **Ask About Programs:** Inquire about special programs or incentives that may be available to first-time homebuyers.
4. **Read Reviews:** Check online reviews and testimonials to gauge the experiences of other borrowers with the lender.

Obtaining a mortgage pre-approval sets you on the path to homeownership with confidence and clarity. Understanding different mortgage options and selecting the right lender will ensure a smooth and successful home buying journey.

Finding the Perfect Home

Now that you're pre-approved and ready to begin your home search, it's time to find the perfect property that suits your lifestyle and meets your needs. In this chapter, we'll explore the essential steps to help you find your dream home, including identifying preferred neighborhoods, the benefits of working with a real estate agent, and evaluating property features.

Identifying Preferred Neighborhoods

1. **Location, Location, Location:** Consider the proximity to your workplace, schools, amenities, and other essential places. Determine your preferred commute time and explore neighborhoods that align with your lifestyle.
2. **Safety and Security:** Research crime rates and safety statistics for the neighborhoods you're interested in to ensure a secure living environment.
3. **Amenities and Recreation:** Look for neighborhoods that offer the amenities and recreational opportunities that are important to you, such as parks, community centers, shopping centers, and entertainment options.
4. **School District:** If you have children or plan to start a family, researching the quality of the local school district is crucial.
5. **Future Development:** Investigate any planned or ongoing developments in the area, as they may impact property values and the neighborhood's overall appeal.

Working with a Real Estate Agent

1. **Expert Guidance:** A real estate agent is your trusted partner in the homebuying process. They have extensive knowledge of the local market, can provide insights on various neighborhoods, and help you make informed decisions.
2. **Access to Listings:** Real estate agents have access to a wide range of listings, including properties that may not be available to the general public. They can tailor the search to match your preferences.

3. **Negotiation Skills:** Your agent will negotiate on your behalf to secure the best possible price and terms for the property you choose.
4. **Streamlined Process:** An experienced agent will guide you through the paperwork, inspections, and closing process, ensuring a smooth transaction from start to finish.

Evaluating Property Features

1. **Home Size and Layout:** Consider the number of bedrooms, bathrooms, and overall square footage that fits your family's needs.
2. **Outdoor Space:** Evaluate the property's yard size and landscaping. Determine if it meets your requirements for outdoor activities and entertainment.
3. **Home Condition:** Assess the condition of the property, including the roof, plumbing, electrical systems, and HVAC. A home inspection is highly recommended to identify any potential issues.
4. **Storage Space:** Check for sufficient storage space, such as closets, attic, basement, or garage, to accommodate your belongings.
5. **Future Expansion:** Consider the potential for future expansion or renovations if you have plans to grow or modify the property.

By identifying preferred neighborhoods, collaborating with a real estate agent, and evaluating essential property features, you're well on your way to finding the ideal home.

Making an Offer

Congratulations on finding the home that meets your requirements and captures your heart! Now it's time to make an offer. In this chapter, we'll walk you through the process of making a purchase offer, understanding its components, negotiation tips, and the significance of contingencies and escrow.

Understanding Purchase Offers

1. **Components of a Purchase Offer:** A purchase offer typically includes the proposed purchase price, requested contingencies, desired closing date, and any additional terms or conditions.
2. **Earnest Money Deposit:** Along with your offer, you'll submit an earnest money deposit as a show of good faith. This deposit is held in an escrow account and applied towards your down payment or closing costs at the time of closing.
3. **Timeline:** Discuss the desired timeline for the offer's expiration with your real estate agent. It's essential to act promptly while allowing sufficient time for the seller to respond.

Negotiation Tips

1. **Stay Realistic:** Set a maximum budget for your purchase and be prepared to negotiate within that range. Understand the local market conditions and comparable sales to guide your negotiation strategy.
2. **Be Flexible:** Be open to compromise on non-essential items to maintain a positive negotiation process.
3. **Leverage Contingencies:** Include appropriate contingencies in your offer, such as financing, appraisal, inspection, and home sale contingencies. These provisions protect your interests and provide opportunities to renegotiate or walk away if needed.

Contingencies and Escrow

1. **Inspection Contingency:** After your offer is accepted, schedule a professional home inspection. If significant issues are found, you can request repairs or credits from the seller, renegotiate the price, or choose to withdraw from the transaction.
2. **Appraisal Contingency:** Lenders require an appraisal to verify the property's value aligns with the purchase price. If the appraisal comes in lower than the offered price, you may need to renegotiate or provide additional funds.
3. **Financing Contingency:** A financing contingency safeguards you if your mortgage loan application is denied or if the terms change unexpectedly.
4. **Title Contingency:** The title search ensures the property has a clear title, free from any liens or encumbrances. The title contingency protects you from assuming any existing property-related legal issues.
5. **Escrow:** Once your offer is accepted, the earnest money deposit is placed in an escrow account. This neutral third-party holds the funds until all contingencies are met, and the transaction is finalized at closing.

Navigating the offer process can be intricate, but with the expertise of your real estate agent and a comprehensive understanding of purchase offers, you'll be prepared for this significant step.

Home Inspections

Congratulations on reaching the home inspection stage! This critical step provides a thorough assessment of the property's condition and helps you make informed decisions before finalizing the purchase. In this chapter, we'll explore the significance of home inspections, selecting a qualified inspector, and understanding and reviewing inspection reports.

Importance of Home Inspections

1. **Protecting Your Investment:** A home inspection is your opportunity to identify any existing or potential issues with the property. It allows you to make an informed decision and protects your investment by avoiding unexpected and costly repairs down the road.
2. **Peace of Mind:** Knowing the condition of the property offers peace of mind, especially for first-time homebuyers. A thorough inspection helps ensure you are fully aware of the property's strengths and weaknesses.
3. **Negotiating Power:** If the inspection reveals significant issues, you can negotiate with the seller for repairs or concessions, ensuring you are getting the best value for your investment.

Selecting a Qualified Inspector

1. **Seek Recommendations:** Ask your real estate agent, friends, or family for recommendations on reputable home inspectors with a track record of providing detailed and unbiased assessments.
2. **Verify Credentials:** Ensure the inspector is licensed and certified by relevant professional organizations. This certification demonstrates their expertise and commitment to following industry standards.
3. **Experience Matters:** Consider inspectors with ample experience in the local market and with similar property types. Experienced inspectors are better equipped to identify potential concerns.

Reviewing Inspection Reports

1. **Comprehensive and Detailed:** A comprehensive inspection report should cover all major

components of the property, including the foundation, roofing, plumbing, electrical systems, HVAC, and more.
   2. **Clear Descriptions:** The report should provide clear and concise descriptions of any issues found during the inspection, along with photographs or diagrams to support the findings.
   3. **Prioritization of Repairs:** Your inspector may classify issues as major concerns or minor repairs. Understanding the priority of repairs helps you plan and budget accordingly.
   4. **Ask Questions:** If you have any questions or need further clarification, don't hesitate to ask your inspector. They are there to help you understand the condition of the property fully.
   5. **Consult with Your Agent:** Discuss the inspection report with your real estate agent to strategize on potential negotiation points with the seller.

A home inspection is an essential step in the homebuying process. Take the time to select a qualified inspector, review the report carefully, and address any concerns with your real estate agent. With a thorough inspection, you can proceed with confidence, knowing you are making an informed decision about your future home.

Finalizing the Purchase

Congratulations! You're now at the final stage of the homebuying journey - finalizing the purchase of your dream home. In this chapter, we'll explore the essential steps to ensure a smooth and successful closing process.

Reviewing the Purchase Agreement

   1. **Legal Document:** The purchase agreement, also known as the sales contract, is a legally binding document that outlines the terms and conditions of the home purchase. Review it thoroughly and ensure you understand all the terms before signing.

2. **Contingencies:** Check for any contingencies mentioned in the agreement, such as a home inspection contingency or financing contingency. These clauses provide you with certain protections during the transaction.
3. **Negotiation Outcomes:** If there were any repairs or concessions negotiated after the home inspection, ensure that these are reflected accurately in the purchase agreement.
4. **Closing Date and Possession:** Verify the agreed-upon closing date and discuss any plans for possession of the property to align with your moving timeline.

Securing Homeowners Insurance

1. **Shop Around:** Obtain quotes from multiple insurance providers to find the best coverage and rates for your new home. Your lender may also have specific insurance requirements.
2. **Coverage Details:** Ensure that the homeowners insurance policy covers the replacement value of your home and belongings, as well as liability protection.
3. **Bind the Policy:** Once you've selected a policy, work with your insurance agent to bind the coverage. You'll need to provide proof of insurance to your lender before the closing.

Preparing for the Closing Process

1. **Settlement Statement:** Review the Closing Disclosure or HUD-1 Settlement Statement, which outlines all the closing costs and fees associated with the transaction. Compare it with the Loan Estimate to ensure accuracy.
2. **Certified Funds:** Check with your escrow or closing agent on the amount and method of payment required for closing costs. Often, certified

funds are needed, so plan ahead to have the necessary funds available.

3. **Final Walk-Through:** Schedule a final walk-through of the property before closing to ensure it's in the same condition as when you made the offer and that any agreed-upon repairs have been completed.
4. **Closing Day Preparation:** On the day of closing, bring a valid ID and any additional documents requested by your closing agent or attorney. Be prepared for signatures and last-minute details.

The Closing Day

1. **Signing Documents:** At the closing, you'll sign all the necessary legal documents, including the deed, mortgage note, and any other required paperwork.
2. **Funding and Recording:** Once all parties have signed the documents, the funds will be transferred to the seller, and the deed will be recorded with the appropriate government agency.
3. **Celebration Time:** Congratulations! You are now officially a homeowner! Take a moment to celebrate your achievement and the exciting new chapter ahead.

The homebuying process culminates with the closing, where you officially become the owner of your new home. Prepare well, review all documents carefully, and work with your real estate agent, closing agent, and lender to ensure a successful closing. Before you know it, you'll be holding the keys to your dream home.

Closing the Deal

Congratulations! You're almost there - just a few more steps, and you'll be the proud owner of your new home. In this chapter, we'll delve into the final phase of the homebuying process, from understanding closing costs to signing the final documents on closing day.

Understanding Closing Costs

1. **What Are Closing Costs:** Closing costs are the fees and expenses associated with finalizing the home purchase. They typically range from 2% to 5% of the home's purchase price.
2. **Common Closing Costs:** Some common closing costs include loan origination fees, appraisal fees, title search and insurance, escrow fees, property taxes, and prepaid interest.
3. **Reviewing the Closing Disclosure:** Before closing day, you'll receive a Closing Disclosure that outlines all the closing costs you'll be responsible for. Review it carefully to understand the breakdown of expenses.
4. **Negotiating Closing Costs:** In some cases, you may be able to negotiate with the seller to cover some of the closing costs. Your real estate agent can advise you on the best approach.

What to Expect on Closing Day

1. **Location and Attendees:** The closing typically takes place at the office of the escrow or title company, or an attorney's office. Attendees usually include you (the buyer), the seller, real estate agents, and a closing agent or attorney.
2. **Final Walk-Through:** Before the closing meeting, consider conducting a final walk-through of the property to ensure it's in the agreed-upon condition.

3. **Reviewing Documents:** During the closing, you'll sign various legal documents related to the home purchase, including the deed, mortgage note, and other disclosures.
4. **Payment of Closing Costs:** You'll need to provide payment for the closing costs, often in the form of certified funds. Check with your closing agent beforehand to know the exact amount and payment method required.

Signing the Final Documents

1. **Read Before You Sign:** Take your time to read and understand each document before signing. Don't hesitate to ask questions if something is unclear.
2. **ID and Proof of Insurance:** Bring a valid photo ID and proof of homeowners insurance to the closing. Your lender and closing agent will need these documents.
3. **Acknowledging Loan Terms:** Be aware of the loan terms and conditions, including the interest rate, monthly payment, and any prepayment penalties.
4. **Title Transfer:** During the closing, the title to the property will be transferred from the seller to you, and you'll receive the keys to your new home.

Finalizing the Purchase

The closing marks the final step in your journey to homeownership. It's an exciting time when all your efforts culminate in the ownership of your dream home. Make sure to review all documents carefully, ask questions if needed, and work closely with your real estate agent, lender, and closing agent to ensure a smooth and successful closing process. Now, you're all set to embark on the exciting adventure of homeownership!

Moving In and Settling Down

Congratulations on becoming a proud homeowner! Now that you've closed the deal and received the keys to your new home, it's time to make the exciting transition into your new space. In this chapter, we'll guide you through the process of moving in, setting up utilities and services, and settling into your new home sweet home.

Preparing for the Move

1. **Creating a Moving Checklist:** Before the big day, make a moving checklist to keep track of essential tasks. This will help you stay organized and minimize stress during the move.
2. **Hiring a Moving Company:** Decide whether you'll hire a professional moving company or handle the move yourself with the help of friends and family. Get quotes from multiple companies and book well in advance.
3. **Packing Efficiently:** Start packing your belongings early, starting with non-essential items. Label boxes by room to make unpacking easier. Consider decluttering and donating items you no longer need to lighten your load.
4. **Notifying Important Parties:** Remember to notify the post office, banks, insurance companies, and other relevant parties about your change of address.

Setting Up Utilities and Services

1. **Electricity and Gas:** Contact your local utility providers to transfer or set up electricity and gas

services at your new address. Make sure everything is in place before moving day.
2. **Water and Sewage:** Arrange for water and sewage services to be connected on your move-in day.
3. **Internet and Cable:** Research internet and cable providers in your area and schedule installation for your preferred services.
4. **Home Security System:** If you plan to install a home security system, coordinate with the provider to ensure it's set up promptly after moving in.

Settling into Your New Home

1. **Unpacking Essentials:** Begin by unpacking essentials like bedding, kitchen items, and toiletries. This will allow you to function comfortably during the first few days.
2. **Home Inspection:** Conduct a thorough inspection of your new home to ensure everything is in good condition and matches the condition stated in the purchase agreement.
3. **Safety Precautions:** Test smoke detectors, carbon monoxide alarms, and other safety devices to ensure they are functioning correctly.
4. **Home Maintenance:** Familiarize yourself with the home's maintenance needs and create a schedule for routine upkeep tasks.
5. **Meeting the Neighbors:** Take the opportunity to introduce yourself to your new neighbors and get to know the community.

Remember, moving into a new home is a gradual process, and it may take some time for you to fully settle in. Embrace the experience and enjoy making your new house a home filled with wonderful memories. Congratulations again, and welcome to your new chapter of homeownership!

Maintaining Your Investment

As a new homeowner, you now have a valuable asset that requires proper care and maintenance to retain its value and ensure a safe and comfortable living environment. In this chapter, we'll provide you with essential tips for maintaining your investment and preserving the beauty and functionality of your home for years to come.

Home Maintenance Checklist

1. **Regular Cleaning:** Schedule regular cleaning routines to keep your home looking fresh and tidy. Dust surfaces, vacuum carpets, mop floors, and clean windows to maintain a clean living space.
2. **Inspecting and Replacing Filters:** Check and replace HVAC filters every few months to maintain efficient heating and cooling systems. Also, don't forget to clean or replace filters in range hoods, air purifiers, and other appliances as needed.
3. **Inspecting Plumbing and Fixtures:** Regularly inspect faucets, toilets, and pipes for leaks and signs of damage. Address any issues promptly to prevent water damage and wastage.
4. **Roof and Gutters:** Inspect your roof and gutters for debris, damage, or signs of wear. Clear leaves and debris from gutters regularly to prevent clogging and water damage.

Seasonal Home Maintenance Tips

1. **Spring:** Check your home's exterior for winter damage. Test and clean outdoor water faucets. Trim overgrown bushes and trees. Schedule an air conditioning system inspection.
2. **Summer:** Monitor your home's cooling system during hot months. Clean and maintain decks, patios, and outdoor furniture. Inspect and maintain your lawn and landscaping.
3. **Fall:** Prepare for colder weather by inspecting and cleaning chimneys and fireplaces. Check

weatherstripping around windows and doors. Store outdoor furniture and garden tools.
   4. **Winter:** Protect against freezing temperatures by insulating pipes and checking for drafts around windows and doors. Regularly clear snow and ice from walkways and driveways.

Budgeting for Repairs and Upkeep

1. **Emergency Fund:** Build an emergency fund to cover unexpected repairs and maintenance costs. Aim to save at least three to six months' worth of living expenses.
2. **Regular Inspections:** Schedule regular home inspections to identify potential issues early on and prevent major problems from arising.
3. **Prioritizing Repairs:** Prioritize repairs based on urgency and impact on your home's safety and functionality. Address critical repairs first and plan for non-urgent upgrades over time.
4. **DIY vs. Professional Help:** Determine which maintenance tasks you can handle yourself and when it's best to seek professional assistance. Some tasks may require specialized skills and equipment.

Remember, regular maintenance is crucial to protect your investment and enhance your home's value over time. By staying proactive and budgeting for upkeep, you can enjoy a well-maintained, comfortable, and beautiful home for years to come.

Making Home Improvements

Congratulations on owning your dream home! Now that you've settled in, you might want to consider making home improvements to enhance your living space and increase your property's value. In this chapter, we'll explore the process of identifying and undertaking home improvement projects, whether you decide to take on DIY tasks or hire professionals.

Identifying Home Improvement Projects

1. **Assess Your Needs and Goals:** Take a close look at your home and identify areas that need improvement or renovation. Consider your family's lifestyle, future plans, and budget when prioritizing projects.
2. **Energy Efficiency Upgrades:** Invest in energy-efficient upgrades to reduce utility costs and minimize your carbon footprint. Consider installing LED lighting, programmable thermostats, and energy-efficient appliances.
3. **Kitchen Remodeling:** The kitchen is often the heart of the home. Consider updating kitchen cabinets, countertops, and appliances to create a more functional and aesthetically pleasing space.
4. **Bathroom Upgrades:** Enhance your bathrooms by installing modern fixtures, updating tiling, and adding storage solutions.
5. **Flooring:** Replacing outdated or worn flooring can give your home a fresh and updated look. Consider options like hardwood, laminate, tile, or eco-friendly materials.
6. **Outdoor Improvements:** Boost your home's curb appeal by landscaping the yard, updating the entryway, or adding a patio or deck for outdoor entertainment.

DIY vs. Hiring Professionals

1. **DIY Projects:** If you're a seasoned DIY enthusiast and have the necessary skills and tools, certain home improvement projects can be rewarding and cost-effective. DIY projects can include painting walls, installing shelving, or minor landscaping.
2. **Professional Help:** For complex or large-scale projects, it's best to hire qualified professionals. Contractors, electricians, plumbers, and other specialists can ensure that the work is done correctly and up to code.

Increasing Home Value through Renovations

1. **Focus on Kitchens and Bathrooms:** Renovations in these areas often yield the highest return on investment. Modern, well-designed kitchens and bathrooms are attractive selling points for potential buyers.
2. **Curb Appeal Matters:** First impressions count, and enhancing your home's curb appeal can make a significant difference in its value. Landscaping, exterior painting, and updating the entryway can boost your home's overall appeal.
3. **Energy Efficiency:** Eco-friendly upgrades not only save on utility costs but also attract environmentally-conscious buyers. Consider adding solar panels or energy-efficient windows and insulation.
4. **Open Floor Plans:** Creating an open and flowing layout can make your home feel more spacious and inviting. Removing walls or adding French doors can achieve this effect.
5. **Smart Home Technology:** Incorporating smart home features, such as a programmable thermostat or smart security system, can add modern convenience and appeal to potential buyers.

As you plan your home improvement projects, remember to budget wisely and prioritize projects that align with your long-term goals. Whether you decide to tackle DIY projects or enlist professional help, making well-informed improvements will not only enhance your living experience but also increase the value of your home in the market.

Building Equity and Future Goals

As a homeowner, you're not only investing in a place to call your own, but you're also building equity in your property over time. In this chapter, we'll delve into the concept of home equity, explore refinancing options, and discuss long-term homeownership strategies to help you achieve your future goals.

Understanding Home Equity

1. **What is Home Equity:** Home equity is the difference between the current market value of your home and the outstanding balance on your mortgage. As you make mortgage payments and your property appreciates in value, your equity grows.
2. **Building Equity:** Building equity in your home is a gradual process. Making regular mortgage payments and property appreciation contribute to its growth. Additionally, paying extra towards the principal or taking advantage of a shorter loan term can accelerate the equity-building process.
3. **Using Home Equity:** Home equity can be leveraged in several ways. Homeowners can consider a home equity line of credit (HELOC) or a home equity loan to finance home improvements, consolidate debt, or cover significant expenses.

Refinancing Options

1. **When to Refinance:** Refinancing your mortgage involves replacing your existing loan with a new

one that offers better terms or lower interest rates. It can be a valuable strategy if current interest rates are lower than when you initially purchased your home or if your financial situation has improved.

2. **Rate and Term Refinance:** This option allows you to secure a new mortgage with more favorable terms, such as lower interest rates or a different loan duration. It doesn't increase the loan amount but may reduce your monthly payments or shorten your loan term.
3. **Cash-Out Refinance:** With a cash-out refinance, you borrow more than your current mortgage balance, and the difference is given to you in cash. It's an option to access your home's equity to fund major expenses or investments.

Long-term Homeownership Strategies

1. **Building Wealth:** Homeownership can be a significant wealth-building tool. As you pay down your mortgage and your home appreciates in value, you're building a valuable asset that can contribute to your long-term financial security.
2. **Retirement Planning:** For many, homeownership plays a crucial role in retirement planning. Paying off your mortgage before retirement can reduce financial stress and provide peace of mind during your golden years.
3. **Rental Income Potential:** If you have extra space in your home or property, you may consider generating rental income by becoming a landlord. Renting out a portion of your home can provide an additional revenue stream to help with mortgage payments or other expenses.
4. **Home Improvement ROI:** Strategically investing in home improvements can increase your property's value and equity. Focus on renovations that offer a high return on investment, such as kitchen upgrades or energy-efficient enhancements.

5. **Real Estate Investment:** Owning your primary residence can be a stepping stone to real estate investment. Depending on your financial goals and risk tolerance, you might consider investing in rental properties or real estate investment trusts (REITs).

By understanding home equity, exploring refinancing options, and adopting long-term homeownership strategies, you can build a solid financial foundation for your future goals. Owning a home is not just about fulfilling your immediate housing needs; it's a powerful tool for building wealth and realizing your dreams.

Frequently Asked Questions

Congratulations! You've made it to the final chapter of the "First-Time Homebuyer's Ultimate Guide." As you embark on this exciting journey of homeownership, it's natural to have questions and seek guidance. In this chapter, we've compiled some common questions asked by first-time homebuyers, along with their answers, to provide you with additional clarity and confidence in your decision-making process.

1. Should I Buy or Rent?

The decision to buy or rent depends on various factors, including your financial situation, long-term plans, and personal preferences. While renting offers flexibility and lower upfront costs, homeownership can build equity and provide stability. Consider your financial goals and assess whether you're ready to make a long-term commitment to homeownership.

2. How Much Down Payment Do I Need?

The down payment requirement varies depending on the type of mortgage and lender. Generally, a down payment of 3% to 20% of the home's purchase price is typical. A higher down payment often results in better loan terms, such as lower interest rates and reduced private mortgage insurance (PMI) premiums.

3. What is PMI, and Can I Avoid It?

PMI is insurance that protects the lender in case of default on a low down payment mortgage. It is typically required when the down payment is less than 20% of the home's value. To avoid PMI, aim for a 20% down payment or explore mortgage options that don't require PMI, such as a piggyback loan or lender-paid mortgage insurance.

4. How Do I Choose the Right Real Estate Agent?

Selecting the right real estate agent is crucial in your home buying journey. Look for an experienced agent with a track record of successful transactions in your desired area. Consider their communication style, market knowledge, and dedication to understanding your needs.

5. What's the Difference Between Pre-Qualification and Pre-Approval?

Pre-qualification is an initial assessment of your creditworthiness based on self-reported financial information. Pre-approval involves a thorough evaluation of your financial documents by a lender. A pre-approval letter carries more weight and demonstrates to sellers that you are a serious and qualified buyer.

6. How Much Can I Afford?

Use a mortgage calculator and consider factors like your income, debt, credit score, and desired monthly payment to estimate how much you can afford. A pre-approval from a lender will provide a more accurate assessment of your purchasing power.

7. What is Escrow?

Escrow is a neutral third-party account where funds and documents are held during the homebuying process. It ensures that both the buyer and seller fulfill their respective obligations before the transaction is finalized.

8. Should I Consider Home Inspections?

Absolutely! A professional home inspection is crucial in identifying potential issues with the property before completing the purchase. It allows you to negotiate repairs or credits with the seller or reevaluate your decision based on the findings.

9. How Do I Negotiate the Purchase Price?

Your real estate agent can help you determine a fair and competitive offer based on market data and comparable sales. Be prepared to negotiate with the seller, and consider other factors, such as contingencies and closing timelines.

10. What Happens at Closing?

Closing is the final step of the homebuying process. It involves signing all necessary documents, paying closing costs, and transferring ownership of the property. Your agent and closing attorney will guide you through this process to ensure a smooth and successful closing.

<u>Additional Resources</u>

Loan Program Information:

USDA:https://www.rd.usda.gov/programs-services/single-family-housing-programs/single-family-housing-guaranteed-loan-program

FHA: https://www.hud.gov/federal_housing_administration

VA: https://www.va.gov/housing-assistance/home-loans/

Section 203k: https://www.hud.gov/program_offices/housing/sfh/203k/203k--df

Conventional Loan Information (Found at Your Local Bank/Credit Union): https://www.consumerfinance.gov/owning-a-home/loan-options/conventional-loans/

Missouri Housing Resources:

https://www.mohousingresources.com/

https://www.ago.mo.gov/docs/default-source/publications/landlord-tenantlaw.pdf?sfvrsn=4%20

HUD/Subsidized Housing Resources:

https://resources.hud.gov/

https://www.lowincomehousing.us/

Housing Counseling:

Help for Homeowners:
https://www.hud.gov/homeownerhelp

Help for Homebuyers:
https://www.hud.gov/topics/buying_a_home

Rental Assistance:
https://www.hud.gov/topics/rental_assistance

Recommended Texts:

First-Time Home Buyer: The Complete Playbook to Avoiding Rookie Mistakes - Scott Trench & Mindy Jensen

Your First Home: The Proven Path to Homeownership - Gary Keller & Jay Papasan

A Buyer's Life: A Concise Guide to Retail Planning and Forecasting - Dana Connell

<u>Glossary of Real Estate Terminology</u>

Actual Cash Value

An amount equal to the replacement value of damaged property minus depreciation.

Adjustable-Rate Mortgage (ARM)

Also known as a variable-rate loan, an ARM usually offers a lower initial rate than a fixed-rate loan. The interest rate can change at a specified time, known as an adjustment period, based on a published index that tracks changes in the current finance market. Indexes used for ARMs include the LIBOR index and the Treasury index. ARMs also have caps or a maximum and minimum that the interest rate can change at each adjustment period.

Adjustment Period

The time between interest rate adjustments for an ARM. There is usually an initial adjustment period, beginning from the start date of the loan and varying from 1 to 10 years. After the first adjustment period, adjustment periods are usually 12 months, which means that the interest rate can change every year.

Amortization

Paying off a loan over the period of time and at the interest rate specified in a loan document. The amortization of a loan includes the payment of interest and a part of the amount borrowed in each mortgage payment.

Amortization Schedule

Provided by mortgage lenders, the schedule shows how over the term of your mortgage the principal portion of the mortgage payment increases and the interest portion of the mortgage payment decreases.

Annual Percentage Rate (APR)

How much a loan costs annually. The APR includes the interest rate, points, broker fees and certain other credit charges a borrower is required to pay.

Application Fee

The fee that a mortgage lender charges to apply for a mortgage to cover processing costs.

Appraisal

A professional analysis used to estimate the value of the property. This includes examples of sales of similar properties.

Appraiser

A professional who conducts an analysis of the property, including examples of sales of similar properties in order to develop an estimate of the value of the property. The analysis is called an "appraisal."

Appreciation

An increase in the market value of a home due to changing market conditions and/or home improvements.

Arbitration

A process where disputes are settled by referring them to a fair and neutral third party (arbitrator). The disputing parties agree in advance to agree with the decision of the arbitrator. There is a hearing where both parties have an opportunity to be heard, after which the arbitrator makes a decision.

Asbestos

A toxic material that was once used in housing insulation and fireproofing. Because some forms of asbestos have been linked to certain lung diseases, it is no longer used in new homes. However, some older homes may still have asbestos in these materials.

Assets

Everything of value an individual owns.

Assumption

A homebuyer's agreement to take on the primary responsibility for paying an existing mortgage from a home seller.

Balloon Mortgage

A mortgage with monthly payments based on a 30-year amortization schedule, with the unpaid balance due in a lump sum payment at the end of a specific period of time (usually 5 or 7 years). The mortgage contains an option to "reset" the interest rate to the current market rate and to extend the due date if certain conditions are met.

Bankruptcy

Legally declared unable to pay your debts. Bankruptcy can severely impact your credit and your ability to borrow money.

Capacity

Your ability to make your mortgage payments on time. This depends on your income and income stability (job history and security), your assets and savings, and the amount of your income each month that is left over after you've paid for your housing costs, debts and other obligations.

Closing (Closing Date)

The completion of the real estate transaction between buyer and seller. The buyer signs the mortgage documents and the closing costs are paid. Also known as the settlement date.

Closing Agent

A person who coordinates closing-related activities, such as recording the closing documents and disbursing funds.

Closing Costs

The costs to complete the real estate transaction. These costs are in addition to the price of the home and are paid at closing. They include points, taxes, title insurance, financing costs, items that must be prepaid or escrowed and other costs. Ask your lender for a complete list of closing cost items.

Closing Disclosure

A form that provides the final details of the selected mortgage loan. It includes the loan terms, projected monthly payments, and lists all fees and other costs to get the mortgage (closing costs). The lender is required to give the borrower the Closing Disclosure at least three business days before closing on the mortgage loan.

Collateral

Property which is used as security for a debt. In the case of a mortgage, the collateral would be the house and property.

Commitment Letter

A letter from your lender stating the amount of the mortgage, the number of years to repay the mortgage (the term), the interest rate, the loan origination fee, the annual percentage rate and the monthly charges.

Concession

Something given up or agreed to in negotiating the sale of the house. For example, the sellers may agree to help pay for closing costs.

Condominium

A unit in a multi unit building. The owner of a condominium unit owns the unit itself and has the right, along with other owners, to use the common areas but does not own the common elements such as the exterior walls, floors and ceilings or the structural systems outside of the unit; these are owned by the condominium association. There are usually condominium association fees for building maintenance, property upkeep, taxes and insurance on the common areas and reserves for improvements.

Contingency

A plan for something that may occur but is not likely. For example, your offer may be contingent on the home passing a home inspection. If the home does not pass inspection, you're protected.

Counter-offer

An offer made in response to a previous offer. For example, after the buyer presents their first offer, the seller may make a counter-offer with a slightly higher sale price.

Credit

The ability of a person to borrow money, or buy goods by paying over time. Credit is extended based on a lender's good opinion of the person's financial situation and reliability.

Credit Bureau

A company that gathers information on consumers who use credit. These companies sell that information to credit lenders in the form of a credit report.

Credit History

A record of credit use consisted of a list of individual consumer debts and a record of whether or not these debts were paid back on time or "as agreed." Credit institutions have created a detailed document of your credit history called a credit report.

Credit Report

A document used by the credit industry to examine your use of credit. It provides information on money that you've borrowed from credit institutions and your payment history.

Credit Score

A computer-generated number that summarizes your credit profile and predicts the likelihood that you'll repay future debts.

Creditworthy

Your ability to qualify for credit and repay debts.

Debt

Money owed from one person or institution to another person or institution.

Debt-to-Income Ratio

The percentage of gross monthly income that goes toward paying for your monthly housing expense, alimony, child support, car payments and other installment debts, and payments on revolving or open-ended accounts such as credit cards.

Deed

The legal document transferring ownership or title to a property

Deed of Trust

A legal document in which the borrower transfers the title to a 3rd party (trustee) to hold as security for the lender. When the loan is paid in full the trustee transfers title back to the borrower. If the borrower defaults on the loan the trustee will sell the property and pay the lender the mortgage debt.

Deed-in-Lieu of Foreclosure

A deed-in-lieu of foreclosure is a cancellation of your mortgage if you voluntarily transfer title of your property to your mortgage company. Usually you must try to sell your home for its fair market value for at least 90 days before a mortgage company will consider this option. A deed-in-lieu of foreclosure may not be an option if there are other liens on the property, such as second mortgages, judgments from creditors, or tax liens.

Default

Failure to fulfill a legal obligation. A default includes failure to pay on a financial obligation, but may also be a failure to perform some action or service that is non-monetary. For example, when leasing a car, the lessee is usually required to properly maintain the car.

Depreciation

A decline in the value of a house due to changing market conditions or lack of upkeep on a home.

Down Payment

A portion of the price of a home, usually between 3-20%, not borrowed and paid up front.

Earnest Money Deposit

The deposit to show that you're committed to buying the home. The deposit will not be refunded to you after the seller accepts your offer, unless one of the sales contract contingencies is not fulfilled.

Equity

The value in your home above the total amount of the liens against your home. If you owe $100,000 on your house but it is worth $130,000, you have $30,000 of equity.

Escrow

The holding of money or documents by a neutral third party before closing. It can also be an account held by the lender (or servicer) into which a homeowner pays money for taxes and insurance.

Fixed-Rate Mortgage

A mortgage with an interest rate that does not change during the entire term of the loan.

Forbearance

Your lender may offer a temporary reduction or suspension of your mortgage payments while you get back on your feet. Forbearance is often combined with a reinstatement or a repayment plan to pay off the missed or reduced mortgage payments.

Foreclosure

A legal action that ends all ownership rights in a home when the homebuyer fails to make the mortgage payments or is otherwise in default under the terms of the mortgage.

Gift Letter

A letter written by a family member verifying that a certain amount of money was given to you as a gift and that you don't have to repay it. You can use this money toward a portion of your down payment with some mortgages.

Gross Monthly Income

The income you earn in a month before taxes and other deductions. It may also include rental income, self-employed income, income from alimony, child support, public assistance payments, and retirement benefits.

Home Inspection

A professional inspection of a home to determine the condition of the property. The inspection should include an evaluation of the plumbing, heating and cooling systems, roof, wiring, foundation and pest infestation.

Homeowner's Insurance

A policy that protects you and the lender from fire or flood, which damages the structure of the house; a liability, such as an injury to a visitor to your home; or damage to your personal property, such as your furniture, clothes or appliances.

Housing Expense Ratio

The percentage of your gross monthly income that goes toward paying for your housing expenses.

Index

The published index of interest rates used to calculate the interest rate for an ARM. The index is usually an average of the interest rates on a particular type of security such as the LIBOR.

Individual Retirement Account (IRA)

A tax-deferred plan that can help you build a retirement nest egg.

Inflation

An increase in prices.

Inquiry

A request for a copy of your credit report. An inquiry occurs every time you fill out a credit application and/or request more credit. Too many inquiries on a credit report can hurt your credit score.

Interest

The cost you pay to borrow money. It is the payment you make to a lender for the money it has loaned to you. Interest is usually expressed as a percentage of the amount borrowed.

Keogh Funds

A tax-deferred retirement-savings plan for small business owners or self-employed individuals who have earned income from their trade or business. Contributions to the Keogh plan are tax-deductible.

Liabilities

Your debts and other financial obligations.

Lien

A claim or charge on property for payment of a debt. With a mortgage, the lender has the right to take the title to your property if you don't make the mortgage payments.

Loan Estimate

A written statement from the lender itemizing the approximate costs and fees for the mortgage. A lender is required to provide potential borrowers with a loan estimate within three business days of receiving a loan application.

Loan Modification

This is a written agreement between you and your mortgage company that permanently changes one or more of the original terms of your note to make the payments more affordable.

Loan Origination Fees

Fees paid to your mortgage lender for processing the mortgage application. This fee is usually in the form of points. One point equals 1% of the mortgage amount.

Lock-In Rate

A written agreement guaranteeing a specific mortgage interest rate for a certain amount of time.

Low-Down-Payment Feature

A feature of some mortgages, usually fixed-rate mortgages, that helps you buy a home with as little as a 3% down payment.

Margin

A percentage added to the index for an ARM to establish the interest rate on each adjustment date.

Market Value

The current value of your home based on what the purchaser would pay. An appraisal is sometimes used to determine market value.

Mortgage

A loan using your home as collateral. In some states the term mortgage is also used to describe the document you sign [to grant the lender a lien on your home]. It may also be used to indicate the amount of money you borrow, with interest, to purchase your house. The amount of your mortgage is usually the purchase price of the home minus your down payment.

Mortgage Broker

An independent finance professional who specializes in bringing together borrowers and lenders to complete real estate mortgages.

Mortgage Insurance (MI)

See Private Mortgage Insurance.

Mortgage Lender

The lender provides funds for a mortgage. Lenders also manage the credit and financial information review, the property and the loan application process through closing.

Mortgage Rate

The cost or the interest rate you pay to borrow the money to buy your house.

Mutual Funds

A fund that pools the money of its investors to buy a variety of securities.

Net Monthly Income

Your take-home pay after taxes. It is the amount of money that you actually receive in your paycheck.

Offer

A formal bid from the homebuyer to the home seller to purchase a home.

Open House

When the seller's real estate agent opens the seller's house to the public. You don't need a real estate agent to attend an open house.

Points

1% of the amount of the mortgage loan. For example, if a loan is made for $50,000, one point equals $500.

Pre-Approval Letter

A letter from a mortgage lender indicating that you qualify for a mortgage of a specific amount. It also shows a home seller that you're a serious buyer.

Pre-Qualification Letter

A letter from a mortgage lender that states that you're pre-qualified to buy a home, but does not commit the lender to a particular mortgage amount.

Predatory Lending

Abusive lending practices that include making mortgage loans to people who do not have the income to repay them or repeatedly refinancing loans, charging high points and fees each time and "packing" credit insurance onto a loan.

Principal

The amount of money borrowed to buy your house or the amount of the loan that has not yet been repaid to the lender. This does not include the interest you will pay to borrow that money. The principal balance (sometimes called the outstanding or unpaid principal balance) is the amount owed on the loan minus the amount you've repaid.

Private Mortgage Insurance (PMI)

Insurance needed for mortgages with low down payments (usually less than 20% of the price of the home).

Property Appreciation

See Appreciation.

Radon

A toxic gas found in the soil beneath a house that can contribute to cancer and other illnesses.

Rate Cap

The limit on the amount an interest rate on an ARM can increase or decrease during an adjustment period.

Ratified Sales Contract

A contract that shows both you and the seller of the house have agreed to your offer. This offer may include sales contingencies, such as obtaining a mortgage of a certain type and rate, getting an acceptable inspection, making repairs, and closing by a certain date.

Real Estate Professional

An individual who provides services in buying and selling homes. The real estate professional is paid a percentage of the home sale price by the seller. Unless you've specifically contracted with a buyer's agent, the real estate professional represents the interest of the seller. Real estate professionals may be able to refer you to local lenders or mortgage brokers, but are generally not involved in the lending process.

Refinance

Getting a new mortgage with all or some portion of the proceeds used to pay off the original mortgage.

Reinstatement

Your lender may agree to let you pay the total amount you are behind, in a lump sum payment and by a specific date. This is often combined with forbearance when you can show that funds from a bonus, tax refund, or other source will become available at a specific time in the future. Be aware that there may be late fees and other costs associated with a reinstatement plan.

Repayment Plan

This is an agreement that gives you a fixed amount of time to repay the amount you are behind by combining a portion of what is past due with your regular monthly payment. At the end of the repayment period you have gradually paid back the amount of your mortgage that was delinquent.

Replacement Cost

The cost to replace damaged personal property without a deduction for depreciation.

Short Payoff (Short-Sale)

If you can sell your house but the sale proceeds are less than the total amount you owe on your mortgage, your mortgage company may agree to a short payoff and write off the portion of your mortgage that exceeds the net proceeds from the sale.

Title

The right to, and the ownership of, property. A title or deed is sometimes used as proof of ownership of land.

Title Insurance

Insurance that protects lenders and homeowners against legal problems with the title.

Truth-In-Lending Act (TILA)

Federal law that requires disclosure of a truth-in-lending statement for consumer loans. The statement includes a summary of the total cost of credit, such as the APR and other specifics of the loan.

Underwriting

The process a lender uses to determine loan approval. It involves evaluating the property and the borrower's credit and ability to pay the mortgage.

Uniform Residential Loan Application

A standard mortgage application your lender will ask you to complete. The form requests your income, assets, liabilities, and a description of the property you plan to buy, among other things.

Warranties

Written guarantees of the quality of a product and the promise to repair or replace defective parts free of charge.

www.ingramcontent.com/pod-product-compliance
Lightning Source LLC
Chambersburg PA
CBHW071118260726
48661CB00006B/2639